CONVERSATIONS
WITH
SURVIVORS

Dear Steve,

I hope you find this a much a lot and you to have it.

[signature]

CONVERSATIONS WITH SURVIVORS

Poems by
Jacqueline Osherow

The University of Georgia Press
ATHENS AND LONDON

Published by the University of Georgia Press
Athens, Georgia 30602
© 1994 by Jacqueline Osherow
All rights reserved
Designed by Betty Palmer McDaniel
Set in ten on thirteen Aldus
by Tseng Information Systems, Inc.
Printed and bound by Thomson-Shore, Inc.
The paper in this book meets the guidelines for
permanence and durability of the Committee on
Production Guidelines for Book Longevity of the
Council on Library Resources.
Printed in the United States of America
98 97 96 95 94   P   5 4 3 2 1
Library of Congress Cataloging in Publication Data
Osherow, Jacqueline.
Conversations with survivors :
poems / by Jacqueline Osherow.
p. cm.
ISBN 0-8203-1612-1 (pbk. : alk. paper)
I. Title.
PS3565.S545C6   1994
811'.54—dc20
93-11652
British Library Cataloging in Publication Data available

For Saul, Magda and Dora

ACKNOWLEDGMENTS

The author and publisher gratefully acknowledge the following publications in which these poems first appeared:

New England Review: "What We'd Say If We Explained Ourselves to Trees"
New Republic: "Relocation," "Sonnet on Magda's Return," "What We'd Do, Emily, If You Came Home"
Paris Review: "Eight Months Pregnant in July, High Noon, Segesta," "Fornacette, 1990, Spring," "Mural from the Temple of Longing Thither"
Pivot: "Poems Talking in Their Sleep"
Western Humanities Review: "Letter to Rainer Maria Rilke," "To Victor Jara"

The author gratefully acknowledges the help of a grant from the Ingram Merrill Foundation in writing this collection of poems. She would also like very much to thank Wayne Koestenbaum, Jeff Rubin, and Barry Weller for their kind help with this manuscript.

CONTENTS

I

Letter to Rainer Maria Rilke 3
A Would-Be Song for David Ruffin 12
What We'd Do, Emily, If You Came Home 18
To Victor Jara 19
Conversations with Survivors 22

II

Sonnet on Magda's Return 33
Fornacette, 1990, Spring 34
Poems Talking in Their Sleep 38
Relocation 39
Mural from the Temple of Longing Thither 40
What We'd Say If We Explained Ourselves to Trees 41
Ponar 42

III

Above the Casa del Popolo above Firenze 47
Eight Months Pregnant in July, High Noon, Segesta 59
With My Grandfather Jacob in Trieste 66

I

LETTER TO RAINER MARIA RILKE

They are propping up your native Prague
With scaffolding, but from some height or distance,
Say the tower just beyond the Karluv Bridge,
You can see the patient gothic walls
Hovering behind the planks like solid ghosts,
Envoys from the aging other world,
With greetings in a subtle, dying language.
Your *untranslated streets* are rapidly
Becoming untranslatable. In Prague,
Only time is comprehensible,
A pageant of mechanical apostles
Who reveal themselves and circle every hour
When the skeleton, their doorman, rings his bell.

Surely you remember one eventful noon
Your parents took you to the clock at Staramestske
As I remember countless giant smoke rings
Dissolving in the air above Times Square,
The momentary halos for a string
Of lighted words and Bulova-promoting
Seconds as they passed. I'd stare and stare,
Waiting for a word I knew, imagining
The burning messages that were beyond me.

Could you name the apostles as they stalked,
Their miracles, their doubts, the things they died for?
Or were you so frightened by the bony
Arm, the harsh emphatic bell, that you
Ignored their distant promise of salvation
And fixed on what they meant to save you from?
My clock never gave eternal time,

Just newspapers to buy and cigarettes,
The urgent complications of the minute,
Two zeros' wild race to fifty-nine.

We were not meant for each other, Rainer.
I only dare to write because you're gone
And all the details of biography—
Your fawning on aristocrats and poets,
Dedicating books to people that
You barely knew—do not really matter
At this distance. I can't help wishing
You'd been kinder to your wife and daughter
Or stayed on as private secretary
To the sculptor, hoarding his advice
And haunting, for ideas, the Paris Zoo.
But you wrote better poems at your patrons'
Castles and their empty summer villas;
Your princesses were eager to oblige you,
To have their servants air a tower room
For your rarified inversion of the fairy tale
With Rumpelstiltskin spinning words from gold.

You would not have tolerated me:
My loudness, my gracelessness, my disarray,
My unrepentant lacking in refinement.
Even in a letter you'd have seen them
But I think you'd have forgiven me my poems;
The general consensus called you kind
And impossible standards made you humble,
Charitable, even democratic;
You'd been chastened by the scrutiny of angels.
Where lyricism failed, you honored dreams.

Mine are what you'd have condemned me for,
The way they waver, move to other things

And rumblings of untried, half-formed words
Dissolve into the sound of savored air
That ushers in my infant daughter's sleep.
Something in that movement in and out,
Its weirdly paradisiacal off-rhythm
Overwhelms my not quite dreaming language
And I am lost to yearning, to desire,
To anything beyond the tiny back
I check compulsively for rise and fall,
The heft of air between its shallow ribs.

Call it love, if you want to, call it rapture.
Call it anything that you can understand.
But do not think I mean to say that this
Is the enormous thing that now divides us
When it is something so much larger that
To name it is to break the lyric's rules.
If I write *history*, will you stop reading?

Because whether we acknowledge it or not
It certainly has had its way with us
And proved that to be inarticulate
Is not, alas, the worst of human sins.
Think of what it has annihilated—
Wreaking not just individual death
Which an epitaph can shore itself against
(*Rose!* you shouted in its face, *o pure
Contradiction*) but the wholesale devastation
Of a continent that fed on dreams
And the century you had the doubtful honor
Of gracing as its greatest lyric poet
In the final guiltless hour of your native
Language. Is it your fault? No historian
Would ever say so. But for those of us

Who, just like you, would rather speak of angels
There's a lasting streak of ash upon the tongue.

So what am I doing in the dead of night
Trying to get beyond these accidents:
Language, chronology, geography,
This thoroughly uninspiring window view
Where airplanes masquerade as shooting stars
And the empty winter branches make black cobwebs
In the moon's thick light, as if the sky
Needed to be swatted with a broom.

Tonight, the moon is shapeless as the moon
I saw atop the clock at Staramestske
Whose daily changes, subtle as the ones
They gauged, I never, in my time there, noticed.
I didn't know that clocks kept track of moons;
I suppose I would have understood its job
If it had come around to perfect circle
But I was not in Prague for a full moon.

I'd caught it earlier, by accident,
On a night train from Guramura to Cluj
In a vision my memory will never
Credit and yet steadily remembers
As pale, gray-white interior mirage:
An instantaneous gigantic halo
That at once revealed and sanctified
The wild, jagged progress out my window,
Rescuing what had to be Carpathians
From the undifferentiated, polished darkness.

That place, whether it exists or not,
Is yours by birthright, the unsettled heart
Of the Babel Empire that spawned you,

A lyric German poet, out of Prague
And taught my grandmother in what is now
The northeast corner of Rumania
To ignore the Latin patois of the farmers
And leave off Yiddish for a purer tongue.

I didn't travel there to look for you.
I didn't know you then, had only heard
Your name. I went to see the place that she
Had come from, and wound up in a cemetery
On the outskirts of the town, eating plums
That had fallen on my great-grandmother's grave.

I remember them as greengage plums
But it's impossible to trust what I remember.
Somewhere I have a photograph, taken
For an old great-aunt, who was incredulous
At my endurance, my devotion, that I'd
Gone *all that way* to see her mother's grave.
It was useless to explain that I'd been traveling.
She didn't understand what I could mean.
To her the cities I had visited
Were markers on a grueling length of track
Whose span of black bars constituted *Europe;*
She crossed it with a placard round her neck
Setting out her route, listing the changes
That would turn Guramura into Rotterdam,
The train into a ship, the tracks to ocean,
And strand her in a shrill, exhausting world.
Whether she looked back was immaterial;
Everything behind her turned to salt.
It was her life's single instance of clairvoyance.

She couldn't tell me where she made those changes,
But if I were energetic I could know them;

It is possible to ascertain these things,
To go to the library and look up routes
Of pre–First World War European trains.
But the piece of Europe that I care about
Is not a simple figment of geography,
The maps, the roads, the trains have all disowned it,
Removed it to the no-man's-land of *lost*,
Like a modern, not quite mythical Atlantis,
Denied the testimonial of bones.

It is a place that once existed and is gone
And the quality of its obliteration
Makes the nature of its plums, its moons
An almost pathological preoccupation.

But still I wonder, did she change at Cluj?
Was it nighttime? Did she sit beside the window?
And were the plums—I concentrate now—green?
In spite of everything, I can't forsake
The raspberries ripening beside the road
I actually walked on, within sight of
The river where my grandmother washed clothes,
Setting of the story that she always told
Whenever we were going to the beach:
How, once, a little girl beside her drowned
Going for a blouse that got away.

She also said that vultures would steal babies
And I imagined bundles borne by vast
Black wings, gliding through the air to nests
Where they'd grow up as if the vultures' own.
When did I realize she meant *ate* them,
That it is possible to float, to swim,
That the *Austria* she said she came from
Wasn't Salzburg or the Alps or Vienna,

Wasn't, in fact, anything I'd ever heard of
Someplace else, was past, was history, was gone?

There is another gothic clock in Prague
With the first twelve Hebrew letters for its numbers.
You can tell what time it is without them
But there's something in their presence now,
Like the news of Hannibal's defeat
In ancient gates of Umbrian city walls,
That changes, at least momentarily,
The landscape, dazzling it with elephants'
Involuntary progress through the hills.

Who knows if they ever made it home?
If there are still a few pedestrians
Who can read the Hebrew words in gold
Beneath Christ dying on the Karluv Bridge.
Perhaps a priest or two can make them out
(They say *Holy, Holy, Holy, Lord of Hosts*)
And identify the letters on the Hebrew clock,
The pieces of the psalms on synagogues
That Hitler told his people not to burn,
To keep one city as it was as proof
Of the expansiveness of his destruction.

When I was in Prague they were covering
The walls of one of them with plaques of names.
Surely some are names you would have known:
A classmate, a neighbor, a shopkeeper,
A man who made your suits, a distant cousin
On your mother's side, through Theresia
Mayerhof, the great-great-grandmother
Whose ancestry you didn't quite acknowledge.

Could you have made an elegy for every one?
Or would you, in the face of this, have left

Off elegies forever? Tsvetayeva
Wrote you, *You are poetry.* You are.
But what could you have made of this destruction?
It's easier to make the angels listen
Even, than the people with the guns.
Who, if you cried out, would ever hear?
You cannot even make a catalogue
Of the atrocities. The list is burned.
The necessary words have been forbidden.

We need a poetry that lets them in.
And not just the historic words, but
The words they use to murder now, words that
Only killers or the dying ever utter.
I can't even tell you what they are
And I have wasted so much time lamenting
The absence of apostles from my public clock,
How it ignored the phases of the moon
But showed the headlines, that I've failed to say
The one essential thing. These stories glittering
Above my head as I strain back to catch them
Are the wrong stories. They have always been.

So who am I to write accusing you?
It was refuge, after all, I came for.
Surely this is nearly neutral ground.
Ordinary death, like ordinary life,
Can't enter, only instants like the instant
On a sunset bus-ride by the river
In my daily trek to work on the M5.
I worked the night shift, a connoisseur
Of the unexpected bonuses of industry:
The thick, opaque, obliterating colors
That seemed to stanch the flow of city air
And turned my botched existence to a highlight

In a cruise-around-the-world brochure
That made me yearn to sail to where I was.

That once, the city told the truth at sunset.
The colors were all weighted down with gray
And beneath them, oil drums and loading docks
Didn't bother to disguise themselves
But held their shabby ground across the river.
It was almost like a victory of nature,
Some rare, chance, sturdy, driving wind
That let us know that we were justified
In longing for another thing to see,
That turning from our windows to a book
Was not, for once, a personal failure.

Mine was the new paperback of you.
I had never read a single of your poems.
They were casualties of what I heard
As a component of your native language,
What, involuntarily, I'll always hear.
I am doomed to know you only in translation
And even then to waver, to suspect
The poetry of what you made it from—
The enticing murderous oblivion
That as I sat reading on the M5 bus
Burned the turning pages in my hands.

And I, the ever-failing one, was gone
And in my place, an imperceptible
Attending angel that you begged to hear.
I heard. That is what I've come to tell you.

A WOULD-BE SONG FOR DAVID RUFFIN

(January 18, 1941–June 1, 1991)

For you, David Ruffin, I would be somebody else,
And you would not be dead of crack cocaine
But resting on the dance floor of a huge blank room
Where I'd just have to enter, breathe and sing
Some smooth elation in a sweet sweet voice
To set your hands and feet and body going

As you would set mine going from the one-rayed sun
Of the AM/FM Zenith in our kitchen—
Mine, my sister's and our opera-loving mother's
Who half-hummed, half-chanted "My Girl" at the stove—
You designed my whole surmise at love
And made my lack of partners immaterial
At those dreary, wall-lined BBYO socials
When you would beg, *Sweet baby, please don't leave* . . .

If I abandoned you, I didn't mean to.
And always, eventually, your loyal voice
Would find me where I was and take me back.
Even in Italy, where I'd run off
On my dizzying affair with higher culture,
I shivered when the first notes of "Get Ready"
Stormed the shabby discotheque at Settignano
Where friends had dragged me on some nutty lark,
And jangled my torso as it hadn't jangled
Since the Woodrow Wilson Junior High School lunchroom,
Where tolerant black girls, whose names I never learned,
Taught me, by example, how to dance.

I believed everything you ever told me,
That I was going to walk and not look back
And, given where I'm from, what I've gone in for,
I'd say that life has kept your massive promise
Though I don't think you meant my self-immersion
In early Renaissance Italian painting
When you said I would leave my troubles behind

You meant I'd forget unfaithful lovers—
But I was twelve; I hadn't had any.
My trouble was Northeast Philadelphia
Which lacked a thing I didn't have a word for
But longed for so intensely that I'd ride the el
Just to bum the vantage from its windows
And scour the local distance for a sign.

Probably, the word for it was grace
Which isn't, in fact, absent now from those same streets,
Their puny fifties' shrubs now overgrown,
The squat twin houses hidden both by leaves
And the thick, distorting hex of being young.

Not that I am so old now; nor were you
Only that it's such a long way off—
Though there is no lyric from your greatest hits
That, concentrating, I could not recover
Among the snippets of Romantic odes
And tragic modern European elegies
Tangled up in folded, frescoed wings.

I turn out to have been wildly inaccurate
In the faulty seminarrative of things that moved me.
For quite a number of unacknowledged years
I spun my heady rhapsodies from you,
As lost beside a gold-flecked mono record player

As I was years later in a watery blue
Chapel thronged by packs of high-strung angels.

They are easier to talk about,
Greater and at still a greater distance.
And I don't suppose I'm forced to write a poem
About everything in life that ever moved me

But I've always admired my intrepid friend
Who spent a good part of his oddball youth
Perfecting Chopin nocturnes on the piano,
But fills his poems with schlocky movie musicals,
SweeTarts, sloppy joes, his sixth-grade classmates
As if he's retroactively making a claim
To something like an all-American boyhood
While I'm still trying to convince myself
That I really have escaped *The Man from U.N.C.L.E,*
The back-to-school ensembles in *Seventeen,*
And the romance series by a woman whose name,
Rosamond du Jardin, I never questioned
(Though I *was* disappointed when the heroine—
So brave in embracing her hand-me-down prom dress
As more classic than the flashier new fashions—
Turned down a millionaire Nevada rancher
To marry—was it Biff?—who lived next door).

I hadn't meant to edit so much out,
To have it seem as if we make ourselves
When, really, not that much is in our choosing.
And even if it were, I wouldn't have picked
A self who'd never listened to you sing.

I only wish I'd thought to praise your voice
Before the afternoon, not long ago,
When it came on with the news on Public Radio

And I put away my groceries on pure pleasure
Until they cut the song and said your name
(Not, as I'd expected, *The Temptations*)
Who died yesterday, aged forty-nine,
At U. of P. Hospital in Philadelphia
Of an apparent overdose of crack cocaine.

They were wrong; you were fifty; I read the obits
In the *Times, Newsweek, Jet* and *Rolling Stone*.
They're all I know of you, besides your voice,
Your face above a tux on several album covers
Which, drugs or no drugs, didn't look much changed
At the Live-Aid concert, not too long ago,
When you appeared, in jeans, with Eddie Kendricks,
Guests of the Philly singers, Hall and Oates,
Who savored every "ooh" and "ah" as backup
And tried too hard to duplicate your moves.

I caught it at my sister's; we went wild,
Not having heard you since you quit the Tempts
Just days before our tickets, with the synagogue,
To see you in a tent at Valley Forge.
I've always thought you wanted your own career,
But one obit at least said you were fired
As impossible for the group to get along with,
Insisting, for example, on traveling alone
In the mink-lined limousine that bore your name.

You were still in a limo, this time borrowed
From a limo-service-owning longtime friend,
When they delivered you to the emergency room,
The driver saying you were in *bad shape*,
Your name and that you'd been *with the Temptations;*
And one final limo—is a hearse a limo?—
(Paid for, like your funeral, by Michael Jackson)
Brought you to the place you're resting now

Which isn't, incidentally, a dance floor
While I, of course, am no one but the ex-
Adolescent girl beside a record player
(In a turquoise bedroom with a Princess phone)
That floats your voice above a neighborhood
Where, otherwise, you still would not be welcome
Unless you brought the mail or some appliance
Or stoked the furnace at a local school
Like the one where, years ago, I rarely saw
Any of the token bussed-in black kids
Outside of choir practice, lunch and gym.

You died about twenty minutes away
(By car, that is, and just when there's no traffic)
For me, then, twenty minutes from where you lived.

Believe me, David, I would take it back,
The sequined tailcoats, bowties, satin cummerbunds,
The hand-claps, arm rolls, smiles, slow, suave turns,
Not to mention those last vials of crack,
The idiotic mink-lined limousine,
The restricted neighborhood, the AP track,
The way we white girls, at a distance, loved you.
I'd take back everything that worked against you
Including, say, the last three hundred years

Everything except, God help me, those recording sessions
And the warped vinyl records in my parents' basement
That I swear I have not utterly abandoned,
Despite my elaborate misrepresentation
Of the two-plus decades since I almost saw you

And the fact that this song isn't really for you.
I don't even know if I've paid tribute
Or used you yet again, this time as pretext

For remembering, in writing, the true believer
With jutting teeth, hawk nose and too much thigh
Who thought you meant her when you sang *sweet baby*
And who, despite her adolescent tendencies,
Would not, if she were here, examine herself
In the aftermath of your self-dissolution.
She, I know, would genuinely grieve,
Put on the record that I couldn't find
In any store in my adopted city
And join in, inconsolable, at *please don't leave.*

WHAT WE'D DO, EMILY,
IF YOU CAME HOME

Oh, how we would bend to kiss your plain white hem,
How we would plunder hallowed ground to deck
A throne for you, to stud a diadem,
To fit a palanquin to draw you through our air.
We'd tutor hummingbirds to coil your hair
With columbine, the jesters' caps draped back,
The chambered faces pressed against your skin.
Would you, for an instant, bask in this,
Before you'd send the birds in clusters on
And return all our jewels to their stony houses?
You'd have pity for each orphaned, chiseled thing.
We know they are not what you'd have wanted.
It's just that we could not come empty-handed
And have nothing copied out and bound with string.

TO VICTOR JARA

Don't ask me what I know and what I don't know.
I only know I want to talk to you
From a chance encounter with a radio
On the fifteenth anniversary of the coup;
I knew your name, I even knew a song
Of yours, but never guessed you'd been among
The prisoners in the Santiago stadium,
That a colonel noticed you and strummed
A taunting air guitar. He motioned to
The playing field and you walked out there singing.

The entire stadium of prisoners rose to join you.
You kept singing while the man axed off your hands
And stood, conducting with your ruined arms
Above the *presto furioso* of machine guns
Your dwindling thirty-thousand-prisoner choir.
It disbanded when some bullets forced you down.

I don't even know what I can say to you.
Not that it, in any case, could matter.
The best I could do would be to wonder
If you were not among the righteous thirty-six
For whose sake the world is not destroyed.
I'm not sure you'd favor the distinction
Though perhaps you'd like the legend's emphasis
On the anonymity of righteousness—
How even they do not know who they are.

It's freakish that we even know who you are.
Usually, in a case like yours
The only living witnesses are torturers.

Who *was* that person on the radio
Who testified that he had seen it all?
And who, then, am I, who write it down?

The poems in question have been there for years.
Anyone who looks for them can see them
Wedged between the endless piles of bodies
In lines that stretch themselves to catch the blood
Like angels holding cups beneath Christ's wounds.

They do not dream of transubstantiation.
The blood will only work as ink in metaphor
And, there, virtuosity has been suspended.
There, you simply have to fix your eyes.
Look closely. They were written without hands.

Forgive me these hands, Victor Jara.
The things that really happen aren't poetic.
Just the haunting is the same; I switch the ghosts
And greet, as visitant from that black world
Where fingers touching keyboards never venture,
An iridescent square on a computer
Flickering across the dark to lure in words.

I've got lines, Victor Jara, where you're everywhere.
Anywhere but in a mass grave in Chile.
The least preposterous is heaven, at God's feet,
Teaching rival music to the angels
And distributing among the ones obliged
Eternally to echo, "Holy, Holy,"
A reckless multiplicity of sacred words.

You twist their tempered lutes into guitars
And try your surest feathers through the strings.
The sound is only audible on earth
To waiting targets of the firing squads.

Thirty-six. Then thirty-six. Then thirty-six.
Each line briefly holding up the world.
Enrapture them, Victor, with a final chord of praise.
Lie to them. Tell them we're aware of them
Or, at least, that we're not so irredeemable
That when at last we find out who they are
We will not know we've either killed or failed them
Or even have to calm some dim uneasiness,
Some tremor in each numb, superfluous hand.

CONVERSATIONS WITH SURVIVORS

One does not think of hats fashioned at Auschwitz
But Fany, apparently, would make them beautifully
With anything the SS women brought her,
Bijoux, dangling cherries, nesting birds
Whatever they'd picked over from the piles
Left vacant just outside each crematorium
A crown from this, a feather from that, a brim.
The SS brought the needles and the thread
And, when she did their make-up and their hair,
The lipsticks, brushes, hairpins, shadows, combs

The cigarettes they gave her outstripped gold
With the essentialist black marketeers
Of Auschwitz. All those fine abandoned coats
With fortunes in their linings made gold cheap.
Her present husband, Sam, deloused those clothes
And traded jewels he slipped away for cabbages.
We didn't need a diamond there, he says,
As if I'll think he made a foolish bargain,
We needed something we could eat, some food.

And Fany laughs about the first connived potato
She hustled, and with her unresourceful sister,
Coaxed into a soup behind their block,
How it made them first delirious, then sick,
And after that, she learned to *organize*
To find the stray undamaged seconds at Auschwitz
And piece them into minutes, hours, days,
Four decades in America, three sons,

Two side-by-side refrigerators
(One in the kitchen, one in the basement)
And a floor-to-ceiling freezer all crammed full
By the time she dies of cancer in a hospital.

She always wears a homemade turquoise turban
Above the failing copy of her face
That she pencils in for hours every morning,
Taking, some days, green pills, some days, red
And swallowing potions brought from Mexico
With attendant tales of miracle reversals
Between visits to the hospital for blood.

She has vast experience of hopeless odds.
On the days she's well enough she tries her luck
At the blackjack tables in Atlantic City
Or she and her survivor friends play cards
And jam the Pennsylvania Lottery
With variations on familiar numbers.
Sam once won a couple of thousand dollars
With the number still tattooed on Fany's arm
(His own wouldn't work; it lacks a digit)
And the lucky error of a young cashier
Who couldn't understand his Yiddish accent
And punched in "zero" when he asked for "four."

On bad days, Fany's sister, Dora, cares
For her, the timid one, who had no gift
For making do at Auschwitz, the one whom
Fany commandeered into survival.
Maybe Dora helped to make some hats.
They'd been seamstresses together in
The snowy Slovak town where Fany, wildest
Of the Jewish girls, had learned to ski.
The first magistrate's wife was their prized client;

With her they left the chest of their best things:
A bat-winged jacket with a velvet collar,
A scoop-necked linen blouse—here Fany sweeps
An arc along my arm from wrist to shoulder
To trace the supple line of her best sleeve.
Schmates, she calls them, only just packed off
Before they had to walk the seven miles
To board the stockcars at the nearest station,

The place where, years before, she had last seen
The father in America who never sent for them
But married someone else, that time had sons.
Fany actually saw him once again
After Ray Brown, maker of banana splits
At an ice-cream parlor in Atlantic City,
Paid her way from Europe when he saw her picture
(A stunning black-and-white—now framed in silver—
With a tartan tam-o'-shanter on her head)
And five hundred dollars to the government
To send her back in case they didn't marry.
Headlines read, "Romance of Auschwitz Girl."

But that was after so many other things
Making big rocks into smaller rocks,
As she describes her killing job at Auschwitz,
The envied, swindled, traded, bartered food,
Her mother's instant death upon arrival.
Sam breaks in to praise the crematoria.
*Before that they would make them dig a ditch
And throw them in, pour on kerosene
And light a match.*

                Fany waits, breathless
To tell her stroke of luck, they needed girls

At the textile factory of *Emmerich Macholt*
She and Dora both were chosen to go:

It was a passenger train, they sat *like people*
(With the SS and their dogs at either exit).
Fany claims she never blinked her eyes,
But sat there, spellbound, as her square of glass
Embraced a fleet processional of ghosts
So real she almost thought the world alive.

Each station stop was like a visitation:
The women on the platforms wearing suits,
With lipstick on, with suitcases and hats,
I remember this like it was something wonderful.
There was a woman in hound's-tooth, beige and black,
With rosebuds on the veil across her forehead,
And another, plump one, in a sealskin coat
Whose purplish-gray umbrella matched her shoes.

They worked in the factory making cloth
And didn't know the war was almost over
Until, one day, Baron Macholt didn't come,
The foremen didn't show, the guards were gone
And Macholt's mansion on the hill was empty.
That, says Fany, is when the girls went crazy;
They ran up to the house to loot the pantry,
Gorged on food and started smashing glass:

Windows, then the mirrors, then the crystal,
Then the massive room-length chandeliers;
They hurled soup tureens at huge ancestral portraits,
Plates, cups, teapots, creamers, gravy boats—
An eighteenth-century trove of heirloom Meissen—
Shattered on its maiden voyage in air.

Kitchen knives attacked brocaded sofas,
Embroidered footstools, bedsheets, goose-down quilts,
Dinner jackets, evening gowns, fur coats,
Belgian lace-trimmed hats on porcelain dolls.
Whole rooms were lost in feathers, shards and tatters
And others disappeared when gilt-edged pages
Leapt from books to kindle piles of furniture
And warm the cheering, gaunt, exhausted girls.

Fany tells me she was not among them.
She watched the fire from a factory window
Where she had stayed behind to cut some cloth,
Sat down at a machine and made herself
A couple of *schmates;* she would crisscross
Europe in them on the roofs of trains . . .
But how could she have seen from out that window
The toppling pair of graceful Chinese vases
She distinctly, almost dreamily, remembers
Crushed to powder on those marble stairs?

She doesn't say she didn't join the others
When they hoisted bolts of fabric to the roof,
Flung them off and shrieked as they unwound:
Paisleys, tartans, pinstripes, spangles, flowers
Spreading out like momentary tablecloths
For elusive rows of victory-banquet tables
Frantically awaiting phantom guests.

They *did* throw the fabric off the roof,
But Fany never actually described it;
It was probably the dull, gray twill of Nazi
Uniforms or stripes for prisoners,
I suppose I could ask Dora, but I don't.
For one thing, I don't like the facts she tells me:
Ray Brown didn't pay that fare at all;

The Atlantic City Jewish Merchants paid it,
Though that's not in the tattered article
With the byline Fany Hochmanova Brown
That Dora brings me from her dresser drawer;
She thinks the magazine was called *True Stories*
And shakes her head over the photographs
(A dark-eyed shoulder-padded bride in tulle)
Then finds the better one, the one Ray saw,
Taken by their friend, a Czech photographer
Who kept it as his shop display for years.

She'd rather talk about the recent past,
How Fany, dying in the hospital,
Pinched the sleeve that Dora'd worn for days
And asked her, *Don't you have another blouse?*
Then Dora tells the same story Sam told,
The time, one Saturday at four A.M.,
Fany made Sam call them to the hospital.
They braced themselves, then found her sitting up,
More lucid than she'd been in several days.
She was dead. She couldn't wait to tell them.
Death and being alive were just the same!
Her things were where they'd been: the makeup kit,
The intravenous tubes, the turquoise turban;
She'd thought they'd all be so relieved to hear it.
But later she was laughing with the rest of them—
To drag them there at dawn to hear a dream.

I was gone for all of this, I was in Europe
And pictured her—despite the fading voice
That wouldn't answer questions on the telephone—
Up, as she had always been, all hours
In the ghostly bluish haze from her T.V.,
Scanning past the talk-show hosts, evangelists
For a gauze-transfigured face in black-and-white

Like the one that rearranged her damaged heart
In a one-projector Bratislava *kino*
And dissolved the tears she'd hoarded through the war.

Her friends used to say that she resembled her,
Vivien Leigh, in *Fire over England*,
And there *is* a likeness in the photograph—
Hairdo? Makeup? Hat?—that booked her passage
On the final ship to dock in 'forty-seven
Just before the "war brides" law elapsed.
I believe she found the crossing unendurable,
Seasick the whole way, something like that,
Afraid she'd look unfit to meet her husband,
But Vivien Leigh or not, she *was* that beautiful.
The rabbi said it even at her funeral,
Describing how for years he'd lose his place
In his Rosh Hashanah or Yom Kippur sermon
When he caught sight of Fany, dressed to kill.

After VCRs came out, her eldest son
Surprised her once with *Fire over Englund*,
But, usually, she watched whatever was on,
A television somewhere always going.
There was probably one on while she was dying,
The transmutations in its high glass square
Like glimpses from a locked, receding train.
Perhaps her own life surfaced on the screen
Less unendurable from such a distance:
The mountains in Slovakia she skied on
With the brother that I never knew she had
Who left but didn't travel far enough.

Let's hope she skipped, as in *True Stories*, over
Auschwitz. Though, in real life, she and Sam
And a group of their survivor friends returned.
(*Auschwitz*, Sam reports, *is only a museum*,

But Birkenau, where I worked, is exactly
How it was. They had it all locked up
But I broke in; I showed a man around,
From Holland, but he spoke a little Yiddish,
The room where I worked. Everything. The same.)

It was after that they started talking;
Fany knew that I would write it down:
Carefully, she spelled out Emmerich Macholt,
Saying *I could not forget this name.*
What she meant was *I should not forget it*
As if she needed to make up for what
She hadn't told the first, *True Stories*, ghostwriter
Who gathered all the facts for "Miracle Marriage";

Not that I set out to be a ghostwriter.
I meant to be a poet, make connections;
All along I've had an end in mind
With Fany floating off the hospital roof
On a bolt of cloth that fleetingly bears wings.

But Fany was so sick before she died
Survival seemed like some bizarre addiction;
There's nothing I can do; facts are facts.
And even if they aren't facts, I'm helpless
Against a woman in a kitchen, drinking tea,
Who tells about a pair of man-sized vases,
Some fabric sailing off a roof, a train—

What does it matter that she leaves things out?
Who is it that doesn't leave things out?
Even I, writing now, haven't got the heart
Not to leave out some of what I know.

I would rather marvel at you, Fany,
In the kitchen, spelling MACHOLT, drinking tea,

Defining *organize* as making hats.
What I need is a revised mythology,
A self-sufficient hybrid of Eurydice
Who earns her own departure from the underworld
Without the risk of lovers looking back.

Who, in his right mind, would have expected you?
Not the woman who must have cursed her luck
To have grabbed the only sewing machine for miles
That belonged to Jews who might come back to claim it
And not even your friend, the pretty wife
Of the (surely, by then, compromised) first magistrate,
The only one in all these stories of yours
I think I may be faithfully presenting;
Who could blame her for her lack of calm
As she finds you at her door and shows you in?

She fusses with the pillows of her most
Elaborate chair, measures, pours out tea,
Dispensing sugar cubes with silver tongs
That turn a brimming pair of china cups
To tiny, inside-out reflecting pools
Where filmy clusterings of milk-white clouds
Vanish under lemon quarter-moons.
Upstairs, housemaids scurry to the attic
To delve among the ousted piles of furniture
And set themselves to dust and scour and polish
While, pressing yet another cup, your hostess
Requests that she may leave you for a moment
And slips upstairs for one last going-over,
Returning with robust young girls behind her
To hand your ghost a chest of your best things.

II

SONNET ON MAGDA'S RETURN

I am the one for whom the peacock feather,
Rescued from a footpath at the local zoo,
Is unforgotten through an afternoon
Of nilgai, puma, bison, llama, leopard.
At me—deprived, unlucky, left at home—
This shimmering thing, this offering to *Mommy*
Is thrust by an outstretched, exultant arm,
Accompanied, in vanishing soprano,
By a singsong, half catalogue and half narration,
Filled with names I barely knew in that prehistory,
That lusterless *before-you-were-born*
When a jaguar and a cheetah looked the same to me.
O, bearer of a gold and green and turquoise eye,
The legend has it wrong. You *are* the magi.

FORNACETTE, 1990, SPRING

For so long, I have wanted relatively nothing
Except, perhaps, this chance to write it down:
Here, for example, near a fire in a cold house,
A wide, full valley out my window
Spread to peaks whose marble reads as snow
And within it and beyond it, captured miracles
Urged on by midair orchestras of angels.
Do all of us have places we believe
Made us ourselves? When last I saw this place
I thought I played a little with those angels.
Even now, at moments, I am half convinced
The brashest of them nod in recognition
And the others only seem so wholly still.
There are no really stationary angels.
See? They've chipped at altarpieces' gold
And etched feather marks in frescoes' plaster
With years of hammering their hemmed-in wings.

Just staring out at trees, I think I hear them.
But I also think, with different ears, I hear
A car. This time round, if I'm alone
I'm promised an eventual return.
I've come here now with *marito* and *figlia*
Who've gone, for groceries, to the nearest town.
Now, I rack my memory for every
Animal I've seen in a cathedral
And alternate the art works with *pasticcerie*
Where I decline *caffè* as bad for you.
For these set months I'm never quite alone.
You're listening even at this table when I speak,
The typewriter's clatter an erratic

Extra heartbeat in your baffled ears
As they reinvent the noisy, liquid dark.

You need certainly not have come here.
I'm the whole of Italy to you.
It makes me imagine tiny frescoes
On the inside of my belly, pale gray arches
Coddling them in stately, cloistered light.
Who knows what you can see and what you can't?
We might be staring from some chapel wall.
Where are we? In Italy? At home?
There's beaten gold around my hair and ears,
Your reckless excess, as you tap the store
Your sister left behind. She, like you,
Was lavish with the gold. For months and months,
Feeding her, I felt its burn behind me,
The fiery skirts of saints on either side.

I had meant to tell your sister this
And other things that now will cloud with you,
How, once, when she was screaming in her bath
I saw again the red, wet, twisted face
I saw when the volcano, my own self,
Had stilled, and was, again, momentarily
Off-balance, wondering who she was, as if
The terrible extortion had no purpose.
But there was the enormous, furious face,
Its slippery torso still attached to me,
Singed by what they call an angel's kiss,
A fleeting pair of lips above one eye.

Listen. Through the valley, ringing bells
Are just unsynchronized enough to stretch
The noon into a hundred eight o'clock
And cuckoos chant the minute, not the hour

With base notes for the more ambitious birds
That crowd into these oaks' unkempt cantorium.
Can you hear any of this? Or only me?
For a little while, I would almost make
Your listening the other way around;
I'd fade into the twittering and bells
And let their near, habitual music speak
What I'm never able to write about your father.

For one thing, he prefers music to words,
Has made your sister an aficionado
Of the tambourines and bongos of the buskers
Who rouse old echoes in these hillside towns
And, for another, it's too difficult to write
About a love that isn't unrequited
And only manages to write itself
In shopping lists and notes about who's phoned
And, once, briefly, on a smallish square of paper
I folded in a box when we were moving:
Ten: fifty-three, eighty seconds, ten: fifty-eight . . .
The nervous record of our final night
In ignorance of love's routine extravagance,
Its willingness to move so far beyond us
That it requires another face, another voice.

The other day, your sister stretched a finger
Toward the ceiling in the town hall of Siena
And showed your father and me the "busker angels."
And while he taught her *zither, harp* and *lute*
I wandered toward the canopied Madonna
And then looked out the window at a hillside
I had just seen frescoed in another room.
What changes then in seven hundred years?
Not the Madonna, saints and angels, not
The hillside, not the thin, exquisite guise

Of miracle in this already teeming world
That weaves within its curving solid greens—
These fields and woods and vineyards here below me—
Elaborate skeins of yellow, purple, red;
Where rabbits leap from battle in the Paolo Uccello
And you, for this brief time, are always here
And angels pilfer grace notes from the air
To herald now, along with shifting gears,
Your father and sister's near arrival home.

POEMS TALKING IN THEIR SLEEP

Poems, when they're talking in their sleep,
Speak in a mute, lyric Esperanto.
We don't hear them. We are sleeping too.
Who knows? Perhaps they outline an escape,
The cunning ports of call in one trick leap,
Or map a furtive shoal, a shifting clue,
The progress of a long, precarious rescue,
Like logbooks from a missed, unsalvaged ship.
But then, they may just whisper to their children,
Endearments, usually, but, sometimes, warnings,
Sometimes bits of tales—a wolf, a cauldron,
A drowsing girl whose skin is untapped snow—
Or murmured catalogues of clumsy yearnings,
Their stunning wreckage glimmering below.

RELOCATION

It is, for me, a new variety of excess,
This kind that happens by the random whirl
Of one imprudent planet on its axis.
Or perhaps not so random. It isn't clear.
All I know is mountains rise from somewhere
To startle listless cities to their feet,
That here I am on a provincial,
Undistinguished, unimagined street
And I have no desire to depart.
Is there a peculiar grace to accident?
Or is each borrowed landscape an entanglement
Insinuating as the white, subtle
Elbows of these mountains as they cradle
In their thin, blue folds a shifting heart?

MURAL FROM THE TEMPLE OF LONGING THITHER

after Paul Klee

In Klee's *Mural from the Temple of Longing*
Thick, dark arrows from each skyscraper window
Head *thither* in opposite directions, into
Skies to which at once the sun and moon
Entice like come-ons to a thronged bazaar.
The arrows whisper, *this is what you are*
And I, who've never liked this sort of thing,
Acknowledge what I'm seeing as my own.
Who can say which is its darkest wound?
That all this frenzied wanting never stops?
That mine are such indulged, such meager, sorrows?
Or that I've known such eloquence in arrows?
How these crude weapons, these traffic cops
Suspend so effortlessly my beyond.

WHAT WE'D SAY IF WE EXPLAINED OURSELVES TO TREES

To think how we've squandered you for fool's gold:
A glinting murmur here, its echo there,
The faint, trickster allure of near beginnings
And meanings dispossessed so many times
They stop their ears while we just call and call,

Gathering up these piles of words as if
The words themselves would cluster into messages
Like tea leaves gossiping in unwashed cups
Or glimmers from the slow demise of stars.

It would not be wrong to call this vanity,
But if you only knew what we were doing here
Before this fairly harmless no-way mirror,
Perhaps you would forget to judge us harshly,

Especially you, so luxurious
In your effortless expenditure of leaves,
You linden trees, so dreamy, useful, blameless
Indulging throngs of asymmetric hearts,
You aspens juggling lanterns on the mountains,
What can you guess of this, our single spring,
Or of the day when, years ago, we turned a page
And pressed the startled pulse of what we're missing?

PONAR

In the world to come, the forests won't have secrets.
Leaves will fall on soil made of leaves,
Stems, mud, sand, the usual substances
And everything that happens will be heard for miles:
Leaves rattling, trees falling, gunshots.
Only there will be no gunshots.
We are talking about the world to come.

And the people in Ponar will brush off the dirt
And return to the twenty-seven libraries
And sixty study halls of the Vilna synagogue
To run the gamut in their youth organizations
From right-wing Zionism to left-wing Zionism
And mimeograph avant-garde poetic tracts
On the beauty of the aspens at Ponar.

Mostly, they'll learn Mishnah and Gemara
At the oversubscribed lectures of Rabbi Akivah,
Who, though he was slaughtered like a beast
In the marketplace, according to the Midrash,
Was not hindered in the world to come
From astounding even Moses with his insights.

Not just the rabbis and the rich will study,
But butchers, tailors, shoemakers, musicians;
The air itself, weighted down with ash,
Will rifle through the aspens' skittish pages
For commentaries on the sacred texts

Derived from half-revealed illuminations
Lost before they could be copied down

Along with murals, stories, recipes,
Chemical formulae, dress patterns,
Melodramas, new prime numbers, poems
Crowded together in the rare, dark soil
That polishes the aspens' tarnished silver
To prepare a setting for the alef-bet

Or perhaps to make each leaf a tiny mirror
To shine, in miniature, an unclaimed face
Dreaming calmly of the world to come
Until it fills with gold and falls again—
This time gently—to its waiting place
And rests its secrets on the cluttered earth
Shaded by the forest at Ponar.

III

ABOVE THE CASA DEL POPOLO
ABOVE FIRENZE

In Amata's tiny kitchen the television
Blares its badly dubbed Brazilian soap opera
From its perch on the front-load washing machine
Beside a hectic sink of soaking pots.
He's supposed to be a doctor, but he sneaks around
With the sex-starved mistress of a mafioso.
Is that intelligent? Would you call that intelligent?
And doesn't even guess the twins are his . . .

Mostly deaf, she has to concentrate to hear
And leaves the local women's chosen fabric
Largely untouched as she pays attention.
During the commercials, she chalks in patterns,
Nonchalantly cuts and starts to baste. Her worktable
(So hastily cleared from this evening's meal
That the bread, two napkins and a spoon remain)
Covers all the floor-space in the kitchen
And presses her chair against a windowsill
Piled with whatever fruit's in season—

Not the window with the sweep of trinket Florence
(That's in an unused, unheated room,
And opened just to see who's at the door,
The Palazzo Vecchio and Duomo elaborate
Trimmings on a faint, misshapen pincushion
Crammed with campaniles' tiny needles)
But the one with the view of distant mountains.
The forests above Vallombrosa? I was never clear . . .

She'll look like a ball children play with on the beach
With all this red and purple on her giant ass

Is her knowing verdict at the next commercial;
She explains that the future wearer of this dress
Is looking, at age forty, for a husband
Neither divorced, nor widowed, nor older than she.
*I tell her she'd better look in the cemetery;
That's the only place she's going to find him.*

*Maybe where you come from, a man like that
Would marry a woman his own age, but not here.*
Then she points to a roll of bluish velvet
And says it's for a friend who has affairs;
The friend claims it's less work than getting married:
"Sex, sure, sex. In bed, anything he wants,
But let that bitch his mother iron his underpants"

I lived across the way in a gatekeeper's house
Of a villa whose aristocratic owners—
A count married to a great-granddaughter
Of a Boston girl who married a marchese
(Her grandmother remembered Henry James)—
Seemed to have fallen on less splendid times;

From my living-room window, I would dream out
On a slightly less expansive model Florence
Than the one Amata shut in her front room;
And, from my shower's window, a medieval castle,
Beyond which, unseen, was a Renaissance villa
Willed, rumor had it, by its bachelor owner
To the last woman? man? he'd ever have sex with
("How could you prove it," we wondered, ogling his swans,
His long, straight cypress walkways, orchards, vineyards).

Amata called my morning the dawn of clams—
She knew when I awakened by my shutters—
Patiently explaining to my vacant look

That clams, on the bottom of the ocean floor,
Didn't see the sun till it was noon.
But I did hear her clucking every morning
As she fed my landlord's high-strung, barren chickens
And the pigeons she was fattening for Sunday meals
Who cooed their dupes' contentment from my roof.

She thought I was putting her on when I said
There were no titled people in America.
No counts? No dukes? No barons? I'm going there.
But still this Communist—*who are these lords
That people should've given them half their olive oil?*—
Felt sorry for the exiled, dead Umberto
When the tabloids gave his last word as "Italia";
She told me with emotion, *Our king is dead*
Within earshot of the tiny Communist club
Below her, where her husband ran the bar.
It was empty, except on weekends with good weather
When the mismatched tables and chairs were brought outside,
Or when the old guard got together a card game
Or the count ran out of brandy late at night.

Sometimes, after Amata told me stories,
I'd joke to another of my Florence friends
That *Believe me, Jackie, I have suffered a lot*
Was a routine Tuscan "Once upon a time"
Even though most of her tales about herself
Were blow-by-blows of rare descents to Florence:
He comes at me with a gadget like this,
She tells of a ruthless ophthalmologist,
A can opener so near her eye I squirm.

But people said her drunkard husband beat her
And certainly the son she lived to praise

Didn't come as often as he might have.
As for her devoted, clumsy daughter,

She deserves a poem of her own, at least,
The way she cooked me meals when I was sick
And stopped off in the village *latteria*
To save my walking down the hill for milk.
Not to mention rushing over to get me
Whenever Fred Astaire would come on television;
Once—I think the movie was *Shall We Dance?*—
I admitted to Amata that I hadn't eaten;
I told her that I hadn't been that hungry.
What a wonderful thing freedom is, was her
Response, *when you're not hungry, you don't eat.*

Was I what Amata meant by free?
(In fact, I'd been too lethargic to cook)
I was writing a doomed novel across the way,
As well as hopeless letters to a friend in London
As much in love with a separatist feminist
(Now his wife) as I was, then, with him.
I'd managed to distract him on a recent visit
When I still lived at a friend's house in the village
Long enough to earn the reputation
(Unbeknownst to me) as the *straniera*
With her legs in the air when the neighbors came
Outside to watch the patron-saint's-day fireworks.

Amata's daughter told me this years later—
I, who'd barely touched a man in Italy!
Though I do remember fireworks as we walked home
On the night we finally did get carried away
And I can't say I remember shutting blinds.

Perhaps this was the reason that Amata
Was so frank with me the very first time we met;

Italian men—let's say things as they are—
Are (forgive me; it's a quote) *pieces of shit.*
She must have been trying to give me warning;

He was English, anyway, and a Communist like her,
But these were things she had no way of knowing.
In retrospect, they were communism's last stand,
My patron-saint's-day lover and Amata.

He came again, this time, to my gatehouse
And we had a single peaceful afternoon
In a *gelateria* on a street so narrow
You had to duck in a doorway if a car came;
Its secret was a terrace with a view
Where we said so little we didn't argue.
We were writing, mostly—letters? hopeful prose?—
While the unripe cherries on the shading trees
Darkened as the sun wound down the day.

Amata's daughter said my landlord's wife
Had grumbled at my shutters, closed for days,
I don't think she'd ever heard the rumors
(She'd have known that I, in love, forgot the windows);
No one in the village would have spoken to her,
Though they liked her irresponsible rumpled husband
Whom my friends mistook for the *maggiordomo*
(He was always on the verge of fixing something,
A fifties *Topolino*, the hopeless furnace)
Certainly, he was irrepressibly charming,
Even if he did think it was all my fault
When swastikas were plastered on our gate
Since I'd tell anyone I was a Jew.

I was American; I didn't keep secrets,
Perhaps that's what I'd gone to Florence to learn

Though I believed I'd gone to memorize
Each jeweled finger on a hand behind a hip
In a crowd of nimble, blue-and-gold-robed angels.

It clearly was a city dense with secrets,
Not just the dimly lit, suspected frescoes
Stumbled into in some empty church
But whatever it was that made those high stone walls
Press upon the narrow, teeming streets—
Maybe nothing more than the bougainvillea
You catch glimpses of from heights like Belvedere,
But it might have had to do with how the sky
Turned opaque, a weird thick yellow, every evening,
The treasure of a schizophrenic miser
Who couldn't decide whether to camouflage
Or flaunt his hoard of undiluted gold.
To me it looked more like something painted
Than the faces I would hunt for in the dark,
Hustled, years before, on still-wet plaster,
And copied so precisely on the nearby streets
I could almost be forgiven my confusion
In failing to distinguish art from life.

I even saw—as attendant to a birth,
Mary's, I think—in Ghirlandaio: Amata,
Who laughed when I told her where I'd seen her,
But not as she guffawed when I reported
Jimmy Carter's presence in a crowd scene
(*The Adoration of the Magi*, da Fabriano,
Any Uffizi guard will point it out to you)
Why repeat a face like Jimmy Carter's?
Amata judges from this that Florence's treasures
Can't be all that they're cracked up to be

But says there was a Mary in her hometown church
Who truly might have been the Mother of God

And I tell her she should look at Cimabue's,
Giotto's, Duccio's, Pietro Lorenzetti's . . .
Until she roars again and wants to know
How many mothers you need for a single God.

I think I took the Englishman to see them;
I know we walked at night through Vincigliata's
Cypress woods before the moon was out,
Two city kids in terror of real dark
And I frightened him with stories of the Mostro
(A Florentine variant on Jack-the-Ripper
Who dismembered couples making love in cars).

When he leaves, Amata asks if he is rich;
She won't listen when I try to tell her
That he's not my boyfriend; there are complications.
*What complications? Does he have another
Girl? That is the only complication.*
To this I merely say that he is poor
And she then asks me what I need him for:
Poor, you can be on your own.

Well, now I'm neither poor nor on my own
And if I eat when I'm not that hungry
It's for the pleasure of watching my two young girls
Refine their expertise with forks and spoons
And instead of taking fat, rich neighbors' measurements
I sit daily with my table full of words
(The way I would describe it to Amata:
Imagine a thousand thousand counters spread
With every shade of muslin, satin, linen.

Imagine if you loved concocting clothes)
Where I try, not only to make sense of things,
But beauty. I remember what I like.
(For instance, now, a cousin's Yiddish joke
About the man who tells his friend his son's a poet.
"A poet, what's a poet?"
                             "He makes words rhyme:
You know: *mazel, schlemazel, meshuge, cluge* . . ."
"From this," the other asks, "he makes a living?")

Or sometimes I remember what I like.
The rest of the time, I'm either a failure
Or poetry is not what I expected;
Here, in the middle of making myself laugh,
Trying to turn Amata into English,

Something I've avoided has resurfaced:
The time she told me that my landlord's house
Had been the Nazi headquarters for Florence
(She'd thought that was the reason for the swastikas,
But a man who drove me home after Yom Kippur
Saw the gate and said, "Your landlord's Jewish?"
The count, as it turns out, was probably right).

Well, of course, it made good headquarters; the view
Commanded all the hills and all of Florence;
They chose it for the same reason I had
But how had I erased this from my mind
Until—what is this? nine? ten?—years later?

And why can't I write a poem without the Nazis?
I wasn't thinking of the swastikas;
I was really trying for comic relief
As well as a slightly less ethereal Florence

Than the one I'm always chasing in my poems.
But the Nazis had gotten there before me,
Which could, I suppose, be pure coincidence,
Except that Nazis do not seem like accidents.

Their having picked my house is like a warning
It shouldn't have been that hard to understand.
A person has to learn how to distinguish
Between people on a street and on a wall.
I should not have written my Communist friend
In my first few bedazzled months in Florence
That the Fra Angelico was worth the starving peasants
Or whoever it was the gold leaf might have fed.
It isn't just a matter of opinion—
A provocative subject at a dinner party:
What do you do when the museum catches fire,
Save the guard, who has cancer, or the Leonardo?
There *is* such a thing as right and wrong.

The rabbis might have used my years in Florence
To justify the ban on graven images.
Someone knew how we may grow too fond.
But even if the pictures didn't cloud our sense,
Certain things simply don't belong to us
And no amount of yearning makes them ours.

At least not those things, not that city
Full of treasures Amata's never seen.
I could probably astound you with an inventory:
Not just names and places; intimate details
Of a thousand dangled lives in the Uffizi
And others stashed on hillsides throughout Tuscany:

The Queen of Sheba and her entourage . . .
Let me tell you, I still see them all

But I wanted to explain about Amata
Who knows enough about this devious world
To help the most observant connoisseur.
Maybe I was drawn to her in the first place
Because, like each one of my grandparents,
At one time—or in one place—or another
She kept herself alive with thread and needle
Or, perhaps, because her hyperbolic Tuscan
With its adjectives yanked out of place for emphasis
Was the closest thing to Yiddish in Italian.

Probably, it had to do with how she said
She couldn't look at Germans on the street
(*Tall, blonde, good-looking*, she'd shudder)
Even the women seemed to her like soldiers
With rifles at her thirteen-year-old head
As her father led them to his stores of food.

Not that my grandparents' lives were like Amata's.
They moved farther than the fifty miles
Between her native village and Firenze,
And did not see, from their kitchen windows,
A single feature of their childhoods' views
(Unless you count the sky and its accoutrements)
Though perhaps, like Amata, they didn't need views.
My *bubbe* certainly preferred television.
Sit down, she would say, *it's a good story* . . .

It's what everybody wants: a good story.
That's what made them mix the drying plaster
With serials of scenes from holy lives

Exactly the same idea as moving pictures,
But we're the ones who move our heads and eyes.

If I'd wanted to do something for Amata
I'd have written a movie with a complex plot
Or even told the truth about my Englishman,
His girlfriend, me, it was a story.

Still, what were our concerns, compared to television
Where HOLOCAUST was showing in Italian?
Amata couldn't speak of anything else.
Did I know what they'd done, even to children?
She had been right, she told me, all these years,
For hating them (though it was wrong, of course,
Every nation has its bad and good)

But what was it about these people, these Jews,
Were they stingy? Why was there a saying
To mean a thing was utterly impossible:
It's easier to make a Jew give up a crown?

And why am I compelled to put this in?
Why can't I just tell stories about Amata,
Who, believe me, asked that question guilelessly.
I was the only Jew she'd ever known.

If I ever find the nerve to translate this
Amata will look up with pure bewilderment,
Maybe where you come from, this is a poem
But here they're full of hell and *paradiso*;
Here, they're beautiful; they rhyme;
And certainly one poet I'm sure she's heard of
Knew precisely what to do with his confusion.

If we do not find our way is it a poem?
If we not only do not make sense
But we also don't make beauty in the bargain,
So absorbed in excavating our details
That we momentarily forget our purposes
And then don't dare to make one alteration
For fear that we'll obliterate our lives?

Amata, if I had a crown I'd give you one.
But since this is no way to make a living
I'm not even sure I have a poem.
If I do, it's the lyrical equivalent
Of the noisy, poorly heated, bursting kitchen
From which, if you ever look out the window,
You do not see a single cultural wonder
Nor could you effect a ground command.
But perhaps you expect so little from life
You'd be thrilled just to be here, in a poem.
You didn't know the things you'd said were poetry
(And remain dubious about *pieces of shit*).
Still, even though you wouldn't want it
And it shouldn't have been constructed in the first place
I would so much rather have the written version
Of the castle you would see from your front window
If you opened it despite the wind and sun
Or better still (but with no strings attached at all)
The perfect, unseen villa flanked with swans.

EIGHT MONTHS PREGNANT IN JULY, HIGH NOON, SEGESTA

Segesta . . . seems to have been founded in 12C BC by the Elymni. . . . It was rapidly Hellenised, however, and was in continual warfare with Selinunte from 580 onwards, seeking the alliance of Athens in 426. After the destruction of Selinunte in 409 Segesta became a subject-ally of Carthage, and was saved by Himilco (397) from the attacks of Dionysius of Syracuse. In 307, however, Agathocles sacked the city, killed 10,000 of its inhabitants. . . . It was finally destroyed in the 10C by the Saracens.

The Blue Guide to Sicily

"... Tell me, Selig, please, what does this word Venus mean?" asked Hayim.

"... remember the strange looking man who appeared a week ago wearing an apron and a red cap, the one who sold licorice cookies and other such things for practically nothing?"

"Yes, so?"

"He was a Greek and there is a whole group of people called Greeks."

"And they all sell licorice cookies?"

"Don't be silly, they have their own land: Greece. . . . They once were a very strong and learned people. . . . And even though they were very learned and knew how to paint, sculpt, carve, and appreciate fine things, they were nothing but idol worshippers serving false gods."

"Venus and Shulamith," I. L. PERETZ

It was foolish planning to arrive at noon
But, in retrospect, it doesn't really matter.
There was a bar, after all, where we bought water
And my husband bought a sun hat for the daughter
We dared not bring, exposed, into that sun
And I thought I'd make it another joke-legend:
Eight months pregnant in July, high noon, Segesta,
The people at the bar agreeing, "She's American,"
Which from them was less judgmental than amused.

It *was* hard climbing in the stifling heat
With my enormous belly up that hill
But probably, the belly stood me well.
How do you approach a recluse temple?
I'd have lost myself as obsolete
If not for my peculiar role as conduit,
Conducting the implausible, attended air
On a circuit of an inaccessible heart,
As if the god they built the temple for

Might leave those tiny, rumbling chambers streaked
With razzmatazz extracted from the stars
Or some other godly gift, say, lunar poise
If it's Artemis (they don't know which it is);
Usually, I bargained for *intact*
In my absurd negotiations on this subject
But resting, lopsided, against a pillar,
I let its sprawled dimensions contradict
Whatever truce I'd made with hope and failure.

I'd never guessed that air could fuse with stone,
That in some miserly and parched terrain
Meagerness could bare the way for rapture.
Once, according to my book, a city flourished there,
So large it lost ten thousand in one massacre
But all I saw was emptiness and temple

And a tourist bus, apparently jammed with people,
Ascending the next hillside on its noon-day trip
To the long-lived amphitheater at the top.

You certainly couldn't say that time absolves
The atrocities that must have happened there;
Chronology was messy there as everywhere
And, surely, saw to more than that one massacre
As successions of invaders made their moves.
But among the things that this Segesta proves
Is that, whatever else we are, we're also dreamers
And sometimes it's our dreaming that survives.
It might just turn out that we're late bloomers

Who could learn something, after all, from history.
I, of course, was desperate to believe this,
Enormous as I was with one of us,
Beside the child in sun hat on the stingy grass
Begging for something like the Io story
Which explained (at Agrigento's Temple of Hera)
How the peacock's feather gained its watchful eye.
I said, inaccurately, that somewhere near
A boy's dissolving wings gave up the sky.

I lied and said he swam his way to shore.
The truth is I know little of these legends,
As a child I had no patience for their nonsense—
People turning into bears and swans . . .
I preferred the reckless child dreamer
(Feared by sun, moon, sheaf of wheat and star)
Who cracked the ciphers of the steward's vine,
The lethal basket headdress of the baker,
The seven unforgiving ears of corn.

I liked, in other words, to hear true stories—
A woman laughing at the child she carries,

A twin embezzling blessings from a twin,
Blood, frogs, locusts, wild beasts, murrain,
The fact that if the sea would part again
I'd be with those culled to wander through—
I luxuriated in their lulling Hebrew
Unraveling in my ears as they were sung
With the murky splendor of a holy tongue.

The first I heard of ancient Greece was *Hellenist*
Which meant that someone like my grandmother
(Who waited every Shabbos for her Irish neighbor
To tune her in to WQXR
And Milton Cross's weekly opera broadcast)
Would, in Hellenistic times, have been coerced,
Herself, to turn the opera broadcast on
And give up the women section's weekly feast
Of gossip in a din of praying men.

I assumed that she'd have braced to die
Like the martyr Hannah and her seven sons.
In Hebrew school, they made us model partisans,
Avoiding obstacles like art and science,
Architecture, drama, epic poetry.
My father did try to push the *Odyssey*
But I objected to the plot as too ridiculous.
In the middle of a war, what lunatic city
Would welcome an enormous man-made horse?

I still have trouble with that section
(I suppose I've retained my childish prejudice)
And much prefer the episodes with obvious
If out-of-context likenesses to Exodus:
You simply turn the desert into ocean,
The golden calf to oxen of the sun,
And marvel how, despite their years of roaming,

The lost, inveterate nomads still don't learn
The underrated art of coming home,

Wherever, as the poet wonders, *that may be*.
In my case, it certainly isn't Sicily,
Though Sicily is not unlike the luckless spot
Where my erratic people got their start—
Same sea, same sirocco, same near-desert,
Same oranges, same capers, same persimmons,
Same centuries of parallel invasions.
The Sicilians weathered theirs with more aplomb,
Acquiring, besides Greek temples, floors from Rome

With fish, reptiles, mammals, cupids, gods
And string-bikinied gymnasts in mosaic;
A hill or two berserk with high Baroque;
And Saracen palaces whose windows arc
Like spiraled dancers' palms above their heads;
And then there are the rash, elaborate hybrids
Part Byzantine, part Arab, part Romanesque,
Whipped up by Normans bored between crusades
To counter any stray, leftover mosque.

This, too, was one of our alternate histories:
How, first, they slew us infidels at home,
Then went to look for others in Jerusalem;
We were taught, that is, to side with Islam
In the erudite and forward-thinking days
When the Sultan's court physician was Maimonides;
We never heard a word about the spice trade,
The sudden taste for silk, the open east,
And learned to regard the term *crusade*

For any kind of philanthropic enterprise
As a threat, like *B.C.*, in our adopted language.

Sicilians don't appear to have such baggage;
Odd for people said to hold a grudge.
Do I envy them? Well, it would be pointless
And in some ways, they've wound up just like us
In adjacent, noisy neighborhoods in Brooklyn
(Of course, the route they took was less circuitous),
The Bronx, Philadelphia, Chicago, Boston,

Then outward to suburbs, for the driven ones,
Some even to houses whose exaggerated lawns
Set off immense facades of pillared porticos
Traceable, backwards, from their grandiose
Contractors through slavers' mock Palladios
(By way of old-world gentry's stately homes)
To the Renaissance obsession with ancient Rome's
Facsimiles of places like Segesta . . .
They're better off in Larchmont than Segesta

And yet—but I've been planning this *and yet*,
As if it might recover every page
Or work, at least, a retroactive camouflage
To take my more egregious errors hostage.
There ought to be more here than this *and yet*
It's not as if I'd say I haven't meant it.
That air did seem to me like other air;
It *could* have graced an unknown infant grazed by it;
I had to disregard that ancient war.

But the past will never teach me what it knows;
It won't get by the hurdle of what's beautiful.
From post-Nazi recordings all I could tell
Was that their prima donna sounded like an angel.
I'd have listened if she hadn't been the Nazis',
Grateful, probably, for such a voice
If it belonged to less familiar horrors.

I'd love to learn from history, but whose?
How do I get past these angled mirrors?

Not to mention the bias of what remains
When it ought to be what's lost to us that's precious.
I'm remembering my mother's uncle's *alles*
As he held a family photograph from Czernowitz
(Forty people spanning generations
Squandered—each one—in a matter of instants)
And the German tourists in the *shul* at Prague
Examining my civilization's remnants.
Old men told me Hitler left that synagogue

Precisely so that such a visit could happen.
One way or another, destroyers win.
I suppose that's why we've honed their art so well.
I, at least, have photographs, a wall
But there are those with nothing left at all,
Unless you count their breath's transfigured air,
Not even mounds of shoes, eyeglasses, hair.
Surely some of them were given to dream?
Who knows what famished stars bowed down to them?

WITH MY GRANDFATHER JACOB
IN TRIESTE

What did I know of you before *TRIESTE*
On the forehead of a train in Venice Termini
Overtook my father's drifting eye?
That you read the Yiddish paper, ate and slept
And worked and read the paper, ate and slept
(The work was tailoring, I've worn the suits
You copied for my mother in the fifties)
And in the only photograph I've seen
(A group shot with my mother as a bride)
There's something of my father's face, my own.

"Trieste," he seemed amazed that it exists—
Or, rather, could be got to by a train
(The way he'd be unnerved to find "Salerno
Beach," as he persisted in calling it,
Utterly accessible, its edges lulled
By the washing of a pale, lethargic sea),
And that was when he told me you had been there,
One lucky Russian-Jewish prisoner of war;
Not only not dead, not even starving
Or even in prison, but in someone's house
(Probably a tailor took you home),
Running errands through impassive squares
Up a spiral of disheveled cobbled streets
Whose jumbled houses braved immoderate climbs
For a vista of the cornered Adriatic.

My father said you never wanted to leave
But whoever was in charge shipped you home

To chaos, revolution, marriage, a son
And pieced-together steerage to America,
Where no metropolis you ever saw—
Despite the nightly masquerade of spires
In giddy evening dress with rhinestone studs—
Could budge the piece of you stalled, out of breath,
On a sloping side street of your lost Trieste.

Naturally, it's there I go to find you
Since, until Trieste, we had no meeting place.
I guess the problem was those two long weeks
In the hottest part of nineteen fifty-six
When the earth, full as it was, held neither one of us,
That is, not in a state you'd call alive,
Though you hadn't actually dissolved
And I, to my mother at least, was palpable,
Pressing on her ribs, her liver, eavesdropping
Which I'd been doing for a month or more.
Think of it. I must have heard your voice
Since she was in your sickroom almost daily.

Is it actual fact or science fiction
That all exhausted sense is stored in memory,
That a needle on a pinpoint of my brain,
Deftly placed, would loose the sound of you?
You could be in here somewhere with me,
Cushioning with Yiddish-Russian gutturals
Whatever people murmur when they're dying,
In your case, jumbled yearnings overheard
Through a window on a courtyard in Trieste.

I meant to have you hemming Joyce's trousers
While housemaids dawdled on the upper floor
Of the house across the courtyard and one over,

Lacing one another's tricky corsets
And comparing details from the night before.

But foolishly, I went and looked up dates:
Joyce left Trieste and spent the war in Zurich.
Besides, the housemaids probably spoke Italian,
A language which, though you embraced its sounds
(Especially in the streets of Philadelphia,
Where, despite the vastly different dialect,
You'd focus in and eavesdrop on Trieste),
Made explicit sense only by accident,
Something like the coffee you'd walk blocks to smell
In the near-narcotic air behind the roasting house
But never drank because you craved a tea
No one in Trieste knew how to serve you:
In a scalding glass with dollops of preserves.

Maybe one time, at the musty place
Run by sisters who'd once dined in Budapest
You drank at the table where, before the war,
A near-blind man poured milk into his tea
And the sisters debated whether eyesight
Or foreignness persuaded him to do it
As he sat for hours distractedly
Scribbling maps of Dublin on his cuffs . . .

Forgive me if I keep returning to Joyce,
But I know ever so much more about him,
And by some European fluke of exile
You've wound up intersecting at Trieste.
It isn't impossible you grazed each other.
How quick were they to send the prisoners home?
He returned, it says, in nineteen nineteen.
Maybe it was you who took the seat he left

(Would Joyce have traveled in a third-class carriage?)
When his sluggish eastbound train paused at Trieste.

Just missed each other. Like the two of us.
Which means, through you, I've narrowly missed
A twice-removed association with Proust:
"I regret that I have not yet read the works
Of Monsieur Joyce," said Proust, at their one meeting,
"And I regret," Monsieur Joyce returned,
Before they yielded to a permanent silence,
"I've never read the works of Monsieur Proust,"
Who used to meet—when he climbed the stairs
To one of his closest friends' apartments—
A man who later changed his name to Lenin
Whose intact body I, myself, might have seen
When I took a trip to Moscow if my tour group
Hadn't visited the armory instead

Where hoards of tiny, priceless jewel-work eggs,
Inlaid by the nimble fingers of children,
Made a fairly solid case for revolution,
Not to mention the enormous turquoise topaz,
Outfitted with platinum and diamonds
For draping feathers on Queen Catherine's horse.
That sort of thing will probably come back
After Lenin's buried like the rest of us—
You, Proust, your near-friend Joyce, your wife,
And, not too long from now, the squandered century
In which (you had no choice) you spent your life.

You could have made a suit for Ettore Schmitz,
Who appears in print as Leopold Bloom,
And, when he writes himself, Italo Svevo,
Elbowed him at stalls where you bought bread

Or nodded to him at synagogue, Kol Nidre night
(Your tailor's mother thought you ought to go),
Where lines of ornamental Hebrew letters—
Not, as you knew and liked them, strung together
To squeeze out your expansive mother tongue,
But in unfamiliar groupings from the Prophets—
Reminded you that alphabets made sounds,

Nothing like the tight-lipped Latin hieroglyphs
That obscured, from every signpost in Trieste,
The slightly stilted wealthy-cousin tongue
You had no trouble speaking, particularly
To the owner of the shop where you bought thread
Who heard, in your squashed locutions, gifts
Entrusted to him fifty years before
By a man he called not *grossfater* but *zayde*
Who coached him until candies spilled from angels
Thrilled to overhear the holy tongue.

But perhaps you didn't go to that synagogue
(Though you might have; it was built in nineteen ten)
Preferring—if you went at all (a question,
Since, like your sons, you didn't trust religion)—
To go instead to a more humble place,
One that's since been ruined. More like home.

Serazh—I picture it with purple cows
And blue-faced bridegrooms flapping unseen wings
When I'm not trying to conjure all the graveyards;
My guess is that they're, most of them, unmarked,
But one or two might even have some names—
Which could—though it's unlikely—maybe lead
To learning something actual about your family.
Not that it would matter. I won't go.
For one thing, it's far too near Czernobyl,

And for another there's that statue of Chmelnitzski
(A murderer of Jews more thorough than Hitler,
When you take into account existing methods)
Much too close for comfort, in Kiev
And not, from the looks of things, at all inclined
To be torn down any time in the near future
Like some fly-by-night facsimile of Lenin
Who, it turns out, should have stayed in Paris,
Talked to Proust a little, written verse.

And you, Jake, should have lingered in Trieste
Long enough to have a tea with Joyce
To whom I keep returning in frustration
Since he, at least, from his sojourn in Trieste
Left a lengthy masterpiece on Dublin
While you left what? Some beautifully made clothes?
Why not an endearing little daughter,
Who, unlike your sons, would have bothered
To ask a question or two about your family.
What shall we make her Jake? A poet?
A fat *caffè* proprietor, serving tea?
Do you think, with perseverance, we could find her?

Let's have the mother Italian, not Austrian,
Maybe one of my invented housemaids;
Perhaps it was you she was talking about
As she stood there, tugging at her roommate's waist
While you cut pieces from the thick, dark tweed
Joyce's elder sister sent from Grafton Street
Into suits he'd ordered before the war.

And maybe your brothers and sisters didn't die,
The ones whose names I don't know. Or their number.
("I think there might have been a brother,"
Says my father on the phone, when I ask him,

"A sister? I don't know, there might have been.")
It's not entirely his fault. You weren't forthcoming.
But my point is: couldn't someone be alive?
Some child of a child who used the corpse
Of her best friend's older brother to shield her body,
Then crawled across a frozen field to railroad tracks
And jumped a moving freight train to Tashkent?

I've heard much less likely true stories;
Why not your sister's next-to-youngest son?
Your brother's eldest daughter? Your first cousin?
That you never heard from them means nothing;
They probably don't remember your last name,
My father certainly doesn't know your mother's.
For a while, I pretended it was Mandelstam,
Since my father looks uncannily like
The photograph on his *Selected Poems*
And I loved the story of his Jewish mother
Dragging him, a teen, to some great editor
And demanding to be told if he had talent
(The poems were dreadful, but the editor,
Seeing how the boy's eyes burned,
Told the mother they were very good).
We could have cousins anywhere: New Zealand,
South Africa, Uzbekistan, La Paz,
About as accessible as my made-up
Half-aunt, the lyric baker of Trieste.

Still, couldn't a dauntless niece have walked to China?
Some nephew caught a barge in the Black Sea?
Or—since it was Italy by then,
And plenty of Europe's Jews hid out in Italy—
Vaguely remembering his mother's stories

Of a brother's tales of castles by the sea,
Made his way, by freighter, to Trieste?

Perhaps they're master-tailors in Trieste,
Your unacknowledged daughter, your sister's son,
Semi-partners in the genteel shop
Of the daughter of the man who sold you thread,
The place in the Piazza della Unità
Where I once bought a necktie for my father.

Every once in a while, you fix their hems
And send them ditties for their children's children,
The very verses you were whispering
While my mother tried to comfort your near-widow.

Did you mean those Yiddish songs for me?
Or were you talking to your waiting ghosts;
The girl so like your lavish-hearted housemaid
Who turned out to be your only daughter
(Dead, at twenty-seven, from a bullet wound
With her straggly, fearless band of *partigiani*),
The green-eyed older brother, the pale twin sister,
The younger boy and girl with hooded eyes
(Also dead from bullet wounds, except your twin.
The bullets missed her; she was buried alive).

You were telling them to join you in Trieste,
Where, from rising cliffs, a spendthrift sun
Scatters last night's jewelry to the sea:
And the things they have to eat there: schnitzel, strudel,
Dumplings, each with an entire plum.

To think you were so taken with Trieste
When just a hundred miles around the coast

Boats like dark sides of a crescent moon
Send quivers through the faces in the water
Of preening lion palace guards with wings
Standing watch on clustered, mirrored domes,
Footbridges, belltowers, drowsing palaces
Lest someone tamper with their watery dreams.

You could even have continued on to Padova
And found the great Mantegna still intact
In the still unbombed church of the Eremitani,
Where Proust, with pre–World War II innocence,
Says, in "Swann in Love," that it *still dreams*.
(Now, if anything, the remnant fragments,
Pieced together on a slab of plaster,
Dream of dreaming dreams when they were whole.)
Then you'd have returned along the Brenta
(Past the garish eighteenth-century villa
Where, later, Mussolini met with Hitler)
To be stunned again by heedless gilded palaces
Wading to their waists in a lagoon

That even caught the fancy of your *machatuneh*,
My other grandpa, Ben, on Eastern Parkway
Who, though uncomfortable on any spot
Not reachable by New York City transit,
Wanted to know when I got back from Europe
If, while I was there, I happened to hear
Of a city with no streets in it, just water.

I saw it waiting through the thick glass doors
A hundred yards or so beyond the platform
Whose train—if it hadn't started up so fast—
My father might have boarded for Trieste
To rummage through old wardrobes in antique shops,

Armoires, photo albums, silk-lined trunks
For a telltale waistcoat (real or photographed),
Smoking jacket, tailcoat, opera cloak . . .

You're laughing now; your job was sewing hems,
Pressing suits your boss made, buying thread.
Not only did you never make an opera cloak,
No son of yours would even think to look for one
Or—thank God—recognize one if he found one;
And when did you ever hear Italian?
It was the Hapsburg Empire, World War I,
All the local Italian speakers fled.
As for housemaids, you never saw a housemaid,
Unless you count yourself, washing teacups
For your tailor's mother's Tuesday afternoons.

Or there was no tailor. You made pastry,
Butchered chickens, put up fences, polished guns,
Laid the new foundations for the prison
Where, next war, they would bring the captured partisans,
Along with your tailor, his feeble mother,
The man who'd sold you thread and all their friends.
Maybe my father's wrong; you went to Prague.

Only you didn't go to Prague. I know it.
You, yourself, told me. It's in here somewhere,
How you scaled the castle walls despite the soldiers . . .
Weren't you, aren't we, aloft there,
Beyond, once and for all, the dusty ground
That would only drag us down with all its dead?
We need some good cloth, a needle, thread;
A word or two, a Yiddish dictionary;
I'm sorry I know Italian instead of Yiddish—

It has nothing to do with you—or perhaps it has
Since you began this lust for ideal cities.

Show me a city where they speak Yiddish
And I'll show green-faced milkmen, unkempt graves.
Even you preferred medieval porticoes
And would, if you could, have known your half
Of the century through literary masterpiece
Instead of by the things that actually happened.
Tell me, *zayde*, can you? What happened?
Or should we just go strolling through Trieste?

It's nineteen seventeen, or better still,
Let's skip the twentieth century altogether.
They can invent computers another time,
Find other geniuses to write like Joyce and Proust.
This way the Mantegna won't be bombed,
The revolution won't have been a failure
And you'll get pictures of your brothers' and sisters'
Fat, increasing families every year.

Did you bring your needle, cloth, and thread?
I was thinking we might need to make a living,
Or, alternatively, two good sets of wings.
I'd like to write a Yiddish poem, *zayde*,
About your lucky sojourn in Trieste
But since I have no idea what happened there
And keep track only of the Yiddish words
That find their way to Webster's New World Dictionary
Some sturdy, well-made wings might come in handy.

I could, for instance, make you out an angel,
Though I have a feeling the Workmen's Circle
Wouldn't look too kindly on its members
Sprouting even pseudo-religious wings;
It's Italy that got me started with angels.

76

I can't remember any in Trieste
But there must have been a couple in San Giusto,
With Christ and Mary and the various saints
Assembled out of bits of stone and glass;
Did you also get strange notions in Trieste?
Because, I'll tell you, *zayde*, I believe in angels.

If I could turn this century's dead to angels
I would leave off, at last, these messy poems,
And see if I could make some lovely thing.
Is that what you were whispering in the hospital?
That what you have to do is look again,
Find something at least a little beautiful,
Manage to unhinge the day from day

Or were you just trying to make your case
Against that raving nonsense of my father's:
All you looked at in your Yiddish paper
Was the poetry section, which was ample;
And the food you ate you turned to pale, gold cherries
Stolen from a pile your mother and sisters
Boiled with sugar to sweeten *shabbos* tea.
It's true you worked. And work is only work
But when you slept you slept on goosefeathers
Heaped up on the ramparts of a castle.
Even in your sleep, what you could see . . .

Who knew there was such a thing as sea?
So many grand buildings in one city?
As for Venice, I have seen your Venice.
There was a picture of the ghetto in the Forward
And I'll tell you something, they all have Venice.
They have it even at the Epcot Center
But only you and I and—what's his name,
The Irishman?—only we, teire, have Trieste

Jacqueline Osherow is an assistant professor of English and creative writing at the University of Utah. She is the author of *Looking for Angels in New York* (Georgia, 1988). She won the Witter Bynner Prize from the American Academy and Institute of Arts and Letters in 1990.

The Contemporary Poetry Series

EDITED BY PAUL ZIMMER

Dannie Abse, *One-Legged on Ice*
Susan Astor, *Dame*
Gerald Barrax, *An Audience of One*
Tony Connor, *New and Selected Poems*
Franz Douskey, *Rowing Across the Dark*
Lynn Emanuel, *Hotel Fiesta*
John Engels, *Vivaldi in Early Fall*
John Engels, *Weather-Fear:*
   New and Selected Poems, 1958–1982
Brendan Galvin, *Atlantic Flyway*
Brendan Galvin, *Winter Oysters*
Michael Heffernan, *The Cry of Oliver Hardy*
Michael Heffernan, *To the Wreakers of Havoc*
Conrad Hilberry, *The Moon Seen as a*
   Slice of Pineapple
X. J. Kennedy, *Cross Ties*
Caroline Knox, *The House Party*
Gary Margolis, *The Day We Still Stand Here*
Michael Pettit, *American Light*
Bin Ramke, *White Monkeys*
J. W. Rivers, *Proud and on My Feet*
Laurie Sheck, *Amaranth*
Myra Sklarew, *The Science of Goodbyes*
Marcia Southwick, *The Night Won't Save Anyone*
Mary Swander, *Succession*
Bruce Weigl, *The Monkey Wars*
Paul Zarzyski, *The Make-Up of Ice*

The Contemporary Poetry Series

EDITED BY BIN RAMKE

J. T. Barbarese, *New Science*
J. T. Barbarese, *Under the Blue Moon*
Scott Cairns, *Figures for the Ghost*
Scott Cairns, *The Translation of Babel*
Richard Cole, *The Glass Children*
Martha Collins, *A History of Small Life
   on a Windy Planet*
Wayne Dodd, *Echoes of the Unspoken*
Wayne Dodd, *Sometimes Music Rises*
Joseph Duemer, *Customs*
Candice Favilla, *Cups*
Norman Finkelstein, *Restless Messengers*
Casey Finch, *Harming Others*
Karen Fish, *The Cedar Canoe*
Albert Goldbarth, *Heaven and Earth: A Cosmology*
Jonathan Holden, *American Gothic*
Caroline Knox, *To Newfoundland*
Maurice Kilwein Guevara, *Postmortem*
Steve Kronen, *Empirical Evidence*
Patrick Lawler, *A Drowning Man Is Never
   Tall Enough*
Sydney Lea, *No Sign*
Jeanne Lebow, *The Outlaw James Copeland
   and the Champion-Belted Empress*
Phillis Levin, *Temples and Fields*
Gary Margolis, *Falling Awake*
Jacqueline Osherow, *Conversations with Survivors*
Jacqueline Osherow, *Looking for Angels in New York*
Donald Revell, *The Gaza of Winter*
Martha Clare Ronk, *Desire in L.A.*
Aleda Shirley, *Chinese Architecture*
Susan Stewart, *The Hive*
Terese Svoboda, *All Aberration*
Arthur Vogelsang, *Twentieth Century Women*
Sidney Wade, *Empty Sleeves*
Marjorie Welish, *Casting Sequences*
Susan Wheeler, *Bag 'o' Diamonds*
C. D. Wright, *String Light*